By Anna Nadler

Copyright © 2019 Anna Nadler
All rights reserved
Published by Little Birdie Press™
No part of this publication may be
reproduced, stored in a retrieval system or
transmitted in any form or by any means,
electronic, mechanical, photocopying, recording
or otherwise, without prior written permission
from the author/publisher.
www.annanadler.com

I AM A GRAPHIC DESIGNER!

I AM A TEACHER!

About the Artist

Anna Nadler is an illustrator, graphic designer and author, who lives and works in New York City. She loves drawing fashion, people, animals and architecture, as well as creating unique logo designs for various companies from around the world. You can view more of her work on her website - www.annanadler.com and on social media platforms. You can also find many of her original art books in her Amazon.com book store, where she is always adding new journals, diaries, notebooks, children's books, gift books, planners and coloring books. In her free time Anna loves traveling, singing jazz songs and spending quality time with her friends and family.

Thank you for coloring this book!
If you enjoyed it, please leave a review
on Amazon.com!

Made in the USA
Monee, IL
09 December 2019